Cooking with Kids

Cooking with Kids

Patricia Taylor

Introduction by Judy Clabes

News & Features Press
Indianapolis, Indiana 46220
1983

CONTENTS

To young cooks . . .

Cooking is a neat thing. To start out with a bunch of separate ingredients, mix them all together in a special way — and end up with something entirely different but very delicious . . . well, there's nothing quite like it.

Just a hint or two: Read the recipes all the way through before you start. My son once threw all the ingredients for cookies together in a bowl before reading the directions on how they should be mixed. He'll never make that mistake again! The cookies tasted like baking soda! Also, collect all the ingredients you'll need and set them out on the table or counter where you'll be working. It's no fun to start mixing things and THEN discover you're out of salt . . . or powdered sugar . . . or vanilla . . . or cinnamon . . . or something. Make it easy on yourself, too, by getting all the necessary utensils and pans together first.

Surprise Mom and Dad or a special friend with a tasty treat you made yourself.

And, most important of all — clean up your mess! That's part of cooking, too.

—Judy Clabes

A COOK'S VOCABULARY

Bake   To cook in the oven.

Beat   To mix ingredients together using a brisk over-and-over motion with a spoon, egg beater, electric mixer or wire whip.

Boil   To heat food until large bubbles rise and break on the surface.

Brown   To cook until the food changes color, usually in a small amount of fat over medium-high heat.

Chill   To place in the refrigerator.

Chop   To cut into small pieces.

Cool   To allow to come down to room temperature.

Core   To cut out the stem and seeds.

Cream   To mix until very smooth and soft.

Crush   To break into very small pieces, using a rolling pin, blender or your hands.

Deep Fry   To cook at a high temperature in enough fat to cover the food.

Drain   To pour off the liquid.

Fry   To cook in a small amount of hot fat.

Grate   To rub food against the teeth of a grater to reduce it to tiny bits.

Grease   To rub a pan or dish with butter, shortening or oil.

Knead   A method of using your hands to push against dough, folding it, turning it, repeating with quick motions.

Melt   To change solid food into liquid by heating.

Mix   To combine two or more ingredients together.

Refrigerate To chill by placing in the refrigerator.

Simmer   To heat food just below the boiling point; bubbles form slowly and break below the surface.

Sprinkle   To scatter bits of food such as salt, sugar, cheese, etc., over food.

Stir   To mix foods around in a circular motion.

Stir Fry   To fry food rapidly while stirring.

Whip   To beat rapidly; to make a mixture light and fluffy.

COOKING TIPS

- Read your recipe (TWO TIMES) before you begin.
- Get all your ingredients and utensils out before you start. Make sure you have everything you need.
- Wash hands before handling food.
- Use a dry potholder to lift pans out of the oven — never a wet one.
- Remember: Things that are hot don't always look hot. If you do get a burn, immediately hold the burned area under cold running water.
- Keep pot handles on the stove turned away from you.
- Turn the burner or oven off before removing pans.
- Stand mixing bowls in the sink as you stir — it saves splashes and makes clean-ups easier.
- Use hand beaters, a large spoon or a wire whip instead of electric when you can. This way, you have a chance to get the "feel" of the batter.
- When chopping, cutting or peeling food, use a cutting board. Cut away from yourself and keep your fingers away from the blade.

Cooking is fun — Do it safely!

SNACK-WICHES

KID-BITS

CONDIMENTS   con di ment   (kän′də mənt) n.

A condiment is a seasoning or relish for food. Which of the following would NOT be a condiment?

Pepper

Flour

Mustard

Ketchup

ANSWER: Flour

12

APPLE SNACKWICHES

Apples and cheese taste very good together. Here's a fun way to combine them for an instant snack:

Cut slices of apple and cheese and put them in little stacks (alternating the apple and the cheese slices) around a plate. Hold the stacks together with a tooth-pick. Stick an olive on top of the toothpick.

To make cheese triangles: Slice square slices of cheese in half. For apples, cut the apple in quarters. Cut out seeds, then slice each section into small, thin slices.

ROLL-UP SANDWICHES

Utensils:
> knife
> rolling pin

Ingredients:
> sliced bread
> sandwich fillings

Why not roll up a sandwich for a change? Roll-up sandwiches make a simple lunch seem very special.

Cut off bread crusts and flatten bread with a rolling pin. Spread on your own favorite filling, and roll it up!

A tasty suggestion: Spread peanut butter on the flattened bread. Add thin slices of banana. Roll up; place in refrigerator for an hour. Then, slice into little pinwheels.

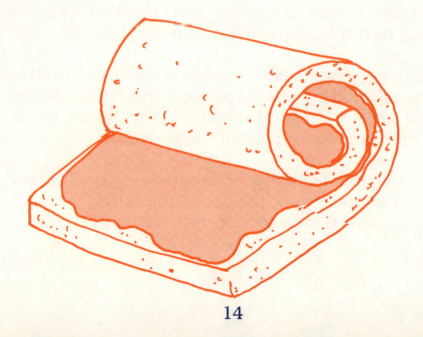

ANIMAL-WICHES

Utensils:
>cookie cutter
>>(animal-shaped)
>
>knife

Ingredients:
>butter
>2 slices of bread
>1 slice of baloney

Butter the two slices of bread. Place baloney between the two slices. Use an animal-shaped cookie cutter. Press hard against the sandwich. Place your animal-sandwich on a plate.

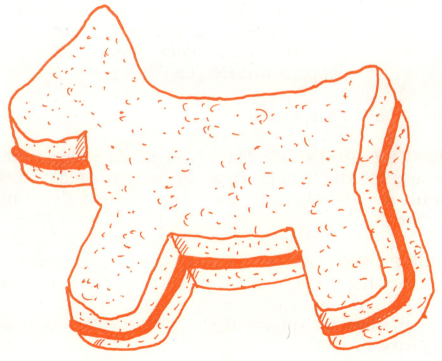

JUNGLE JAUNT

It's a real treat to make sandwiches and snacks that look like animals. Invite your friends over for lunch and all of you can fix these nutritious goodies together. Just get everything ready before your friends arrive.

Utensils:
> round cookie cutters
> table knives
> paring knife

Ingredients:
> sliced bread
> sandwich fillings (egg salad, tuna salad, peanut butter — your favorites)
> sandwich decorations (choose from olives, carrots, radishes, hard-boiled eggs, zucchini squash, cucumbers, celery, pimentos, pickles, pickle relish, raisins, green peppers, string beans, cherry tomatoes, mushrooms, cheese, red peppers, pretzels, cauliflower)

Now, create a sandwich!

MONKEY BUSINESS: Make a regular sandwich, remove crust and trim to shape. Use a slice of red pepper for the mouth, raisins for the eyes, and slices of cucumber for the ears.

PLUMP PUMA: Make a regular sandwich, trim it to circular shape. Use straight pretzels for the whiskers, olive or egg slices for the eyes, tomato and green-pepper slices for the mouth, and cheese for the nose and ears.

MAKE-A-FACE: Surprise your friends with some funny-face sandwiches for lunch! Cut out circles of bread with a round cookie cutter; make your sandwiches using your favorite fillings. Cut each sandwich in half. Put the eyes and nose on one half and the mouth on the other half, using raisins, nuts, hard-boiled egg slices, cheese, or pieces of raw vegetables. Now, mix and match the two halves!

FLOWER-GARDEN: To make pretty flowers that will cheer you on a rainy day, just cut out circles of bread with the round cookie cutter and make sandwiches using your favorite fillings. Then, decorate. For flower petals, use slices of radishes, carrots, red pepper, tomatoes, hard-boiled egg whites or cauliflower. Mash a hard egg yolk with a fork and sprinkle in the middle of the petals for a nice flower center. Cut leaves and stems from celery or green pepper or use whole string beans or a piece of parsley.

Now that you have the idea, create your own. Use your imagination!

17

PAPOOSES

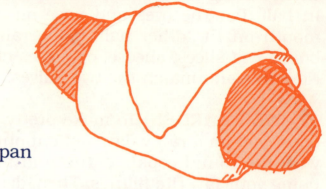

Utensils:
>knife
>baking pan

Ingredients:
>1 8-ounce can crescent rolls
>8 pre-cooked sausage links or 4 wieners
>cut in half

Wrap one crescent roll around each sausage link. Place on baking pan so they don't touch. Bake at 350 degrees 10-12 minutes or until brown.

PIZZA MUFFINS

Utensils:
> knife
> cookie sheet or small baking pan

Ingredients:
> English muffin
> butter
> pizza sauce
> powdered oregano
> shredded American cheese
> grated Parmesan cheese

Split and butter muffin. Toast muffin under broiler. Spread with pizza sauce. Add a dash of oregano. Sprinkle with shredded cheese and a dash of Parmesan. Toast under the broiler until the cheese is melted. (Watch it! It won't take long!)

One muffin feeds one hungry child!

CRACKERWITCH CASTLE

This witch's castle is a great nibbling treat when you're reading or watching TV with your friends. Just start munching at the top and work your way down.

To build a Crackerwitch Castle, all you need are round crackers and cheese. Put a piece of cheese on a cracker, add another cracker and keep stacking this way until the castle is as high as you want it to be. At the top, make a "tower" of cheese with olives around the edge.

SUPER SALADS

KID-BITS

CALCIUM   cal ci um   (kal′sē əm) n.

A metallic chemical essential to the building of healthy bones and teeth.

Many foods contain calcium, but some foods are a better source of calcium than others. From the following pairs, choose the food that is the best source of calcium:

Sherbet	Yogurt
Broccoli	Celery
Salmon	Pork
Raisins	Grapes

ANSWERS: Yogurt, Broccoli, Salmon, and Raisins.

KID-BITS

IRON   i-ron   (ī árn) n.

Iron is a metallic chemical vital to plant and animal life.

Three of the following foods are good sources for iron. Which are they?

> Spinach, 1 cup
>
> Apple, 1 medium
>
> Raisins, 1 cup
>
> Clams, 3 ounces

ANSWER: Clams have 5.2 grams of iron; raisins, 5.1 grams; spinach, 4.3 grams. The apple has only .4 grams.

23

LICKETY STICKS

Utensils:
> table knife
> paring knife

Ingredients:
> 1 celery stalk
> cream cheese
> pecan pieces

Wash and pat dry the celery. Cut off the leafy top and white root section. (Save these for making soup later.) Cut the celery into 4 pieces. Using a table knife, fill the hollow section of each celery piece with cream cheese. Press on the nuts.

Variations: Use a banana instead of celery. Use peanut butter or mild cheddar cheese spread for the filling. Use raisins instead of pecans.

HANDY APPLE

Utensils:
>   paring knife
>   spoon

Ingredients:
>   1 apple
>   1 tablespoon peanut butter
>   ¼ cup raisins

Wash and pat dry the apple. Remove the core to leave a hole in the middle of the apple. Mix some peanut butter with raisins and stuff this mixture into the hole, using a small spoon. Slice it up or eat it whole!

Variation: Use a mixture of granola and peanut butter to fill the apple; use crunchy peanut butter and a small bit of honey or jelly. USE YOUR IMAGINATION!

CATERPILLAR SALAD

(1 serving)

Utensils:
>   plate
>   paring knife
>   table knife

Ingredients:
>   1 peeled banana
>   1 fresh pear
>   1 lettuce leaf
>   2 pecans

Wash and pat dry the lettuce and lay on a plate. Wash and pat dry the pear. Cut it into slices and throw away the stem and core. Make several cuts in the banana with a table knife, then place it on top of the lettuce. Push the pear slices into the cuts, green side up. Push pecans in at one end of the banana for eyes.

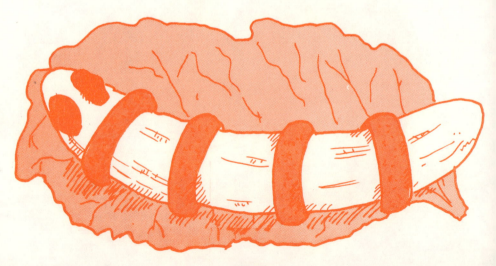

BUNNY SALAD

Utensils:
> plate
> paring knife

Ingredients:
> 1 lettuce leaf
> 1 orange, peeled and sectioned
> 1 canned pear half
> 1 maraschino cherry

Put the lettuce leaf on a plate. Put 1 canned pear half, cut side down, on the lettuce. Add 4 orange sections for ears. Cut the maraschino cherry into 6 slices. Use these for eyes, nose, mouth and inside of ears.

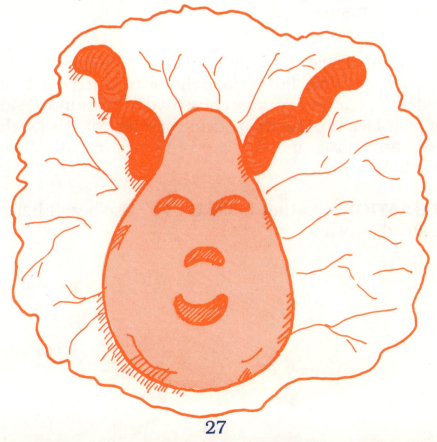

PETER RABBIT SALAD

Utensils:
>salad plates
>spoon
>can opener

Ingredients:
>lettuce leaves
>4 pear halves
>>(one half for each person)
>4 maraschino cherries
>8 whole pecans
>4 tablespoons small curd cottage cheese
>raisins

Open can of pear halves and drain the juice. Put lettuce leaf on each plate. Put cottage cheese in center of lettuce leaf. Put pear over cottage cheese with the rounded side of pear face up. Use the pecans for ears, raisins for the eyes and nose, and the cherry for the mouth. Yield: 4 salads.

VARIATIONS: Rather make ducks? Use peach halves instead of pears.

RAGGEDY ANDY SALAD

(1 serving)

Utensils:
>   table knife

Ingredients:
>   1 ruffled leaf of lettuce
>   1 canned peach half
>   4 celery sticks
>   1 egg, hard boiled, peeled and cut in half
>   (save the other half for an egg sandwich
>   of another "Annie")
>   1 maraschino cherry
>   1 small carrot, peeled and grated
>   10 raisins

Wash and pat dry the lettuce leaf and place on a plate.
Put together "Andy" from the rest of the ingredients:

>   Body: peach half
>   Arms and Legs: celery sticks
>   Head: egg
>   Mouth: celery
>   Hair: carrot
>   Eyes, Nose, Hands, Feet and Buttons: raisins

BANANA PEOPLE

Utensils:
- small mixing bowl
- spoon
- rolling pin
- table knife
- measuring spoon
- salad plates

Ingredients:
- 4 bananas
- 8 marshmallows
- 1 tablespoon orange juice
- 1 tablespoon mayonnaise
- crushed salted peanuts
- 10 maraschino cherries
- 4 lettuce leaves

Peel and slice each banana lengthwise and then in half. Stir orange juice and mayonnaise until smooth. Spread mayonnaise mixture on each banana slice. Use the banana slices to form the legs and arms of your "people." Use the marshmallows for the stomach and heads of each "person." Use the cherries cut in half for the hands, feet and hat for each of your "people." Put a lettuce leaf on each of 4 salad plates. Next, form your "people" using the bananas, marshmallows and cherries. Sprinkle nuts over the banana slices. Use raisins for the nose and eyes. Use a small piece of the cherry for the mouth. (To crush peanuts, place them on a board and roll with rolling pin until they are broken.) Yield: 4 banana people.

SNAKEY SNACK

Make a colorful snake with alternating slices of carrots and zucchini or cucumber. Spread soft cream cheese between the slices to stick them together. Make it as long and as curly as you wish!

VEGGIE INVENTIONS

This is a recipe YOU invent. Start by using the suggestions; then go on to make your own creations! Assemble your "people" by using toothpicks to attach various vegetable pieces and cheese cubes to a larger vegetable "body." Spread the top of the head with mayonnaise and press on sprouts for hair. Add some crazy details, securing them with mayonnaise or toothpicks.

Suggested bodies:
> a small whole carrot
> a small bunch of broccoli or cauliflower
> a cucumber or zucchini
>> (whole or cut width-wise)

Suggested arms and legs:
> cheese cubes or sticks
> carrot, celery, turnip, green or red pepper
>> slices

Suggested heads:
> whole cherry tomatoes
> whole radishes
> large pitted olives

Suggested details:
> Eyes: olives
> Nose, Feet, Hands: cheese cubes
> Mouth: carrot or green pepper slice

Miscellaneous:
> Mayonnaise
> Alfalfa Sprouts

NOW, ASSEMBLE YOUR OWN PEOPLE!

APPLE-ICIOUS

Utensils:
> paring knife
> spoon
> bowl

Ingredients:
> 3 apples
> ½ cup chopped nuts
> ½ cup raisins
> 2 stalks celery, chopped
> ¾ cup mayonnaise or salad dressing

Cut apples to remove seeds. Chop apples into small pieces. Place in bowl. Add nuts, raisins, chopped-up celery, and the salad dressing. Mix well.

LISA'S FINGER TREATS

Utensils:

      large bowl
      mixing spoon
      15 x 10½ inch pan
      cookie cutters

Ingredients:

      4 envelopes unflavored gelatin
      3 3-ounce packages gelatin (any flavor)
      5 cups boiling water

Combine gelatins in a large bowl. Add boiling water and stir until completely dissolved. Pour into the 15 x 10½ inch pan and chill until firm. Use small cookie cutters and cut into shapes or cut in squares, if you wish.

Note: This is a favorite class project with young children. Make shamrocks with lime-flavored gelatin or hearts with strawberry, cherry, etc. Suitable for any special occasion.

SOUP-ER SOUPS

KID-BITS

PROTEIN   prō′tēn   n.

Proteins occur in all animal and vegetable matter and are essential to your diet.

Which of the following foods contain the most protein? Choose two:

Tuna, 3 ounces
Bologna, 1 slice
Sausage, 1 link
Chicken, 6 ounces

ANSWER: Tuna (24 grams) and Chicken (42 grams). The bologna and sausage would have 3 grams and 2 grams, respectively.

CHICKEN SOUP

Utensils:
>large kettle
>stirring spoon
>knife
>chopping board

Ingredients:
>1 whole chicken, about 2-3 pounds
>4 stalks celery (including leaves)
>1 onion
>2 cups noodles
>1 teaspoon salt
>1 teaspoon pepper

Chop celery, leaves, and onion. Put chicken in pot and cover with water. Add salt, pepper, chopped onion, celery and leaves. Bring to a boil (about 2 hours). Turn heat down and simmer until chicken is tender. Remove from heat and let cool. Strain broth and save for cooking chicken and noodles. Remove bones and skin from chicken and cut it up. Add noodles, chicken to chicken broth and cook until noodles are tender.

Make this soup for Mom when she has a cold!

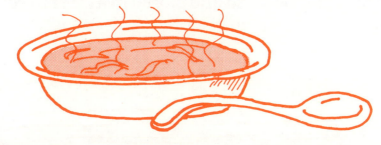

AND, if you want to be really industrious, try this recipe for making your own noodles:

NOODLES

Utensils:

       flour sifter
       knife or noodle cutter
       mixing bowl
       cutting board
       measuring cup and spoons

Ingredients:

       2 eggs
       2 cups flour
       1 teaspoon salt
       2 egg shells of water

Sift flour and salt into a mixing bowl. Break two eggs and add to flour mixture. Fill the egg shell with water two times and add to flour mixture. Stir flour, eggs, and water together. Mixture will be stiff and sticky. With hands, form the mixture into a ball. Flour cutting board with about a half cup of flour. Roll noodles out on board until round and flat — about ⅛ inch thick. Cut with a knife into narrow strips or use noodle cutter. Let noodles dry. Add them to your boiling soup liquid. Lower the heat and cook about 12-15 minutes.

Noodles may be dried and stored in a covered container or plastic bag.

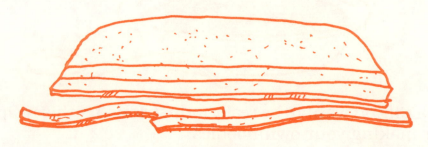

JUNGLE STEW

Utensils:

     knife
     soup pot
     measuring cup
     skillet

Ingredients:

     2 pounds hamburger or 4 cups leftover meat
     2 onions, peeled and sliced
     ¼ cup uncooked macaroni
     3 15-ounce cans cooked kidney beans
          (optional)
     salt and pepper
     2 1-pound - 3-ounce cans tomatoes

Brown onions and meat in fat in a skillet. Boil macaroni until tender; drain. Combine all ingredients in pot and simmer for 20 minutes.

39

CHILI

Utensils:

     large soup pot (4-quart)
     knife
     wooden spoon
     can opener
     measuring spoons
     measuring cup

Ingredients:

     1 pound ground beef
     1 small onion
     1 small green pepper
     1 clove garlic
     1 pint tomato juice
     1-pound can red beans
     1 tablespoon chili powder
     1 tablespoon sugar
     1 teaspoon salt

Chop onion; peel clove of garlic (a clove is just one section of the garlic pad) and chop in small pieces. Brown ground beef, chopped onion and chopped garlic. Drain off fat CAREFULLY. Chop the green pepper. Add the rest of the ingredients to the meat mixture and simmer for about an hour. Stir frequently so that beans and meat don't stick to the soup pot.

ONION SOUP

Utensils:

> skillet
> knife
> spatula
> soup pot
> spoon

Ingredients:

> 6 beef bouillon cubes
> 5 cups water
> 2 medium onions, sliced
> ½ stick margarine or butter
> croutons or toasted bread, cut in cubes
> Parmesan cheese

Put five cups of water in soup pot to boil. Dissolve the six bouillon cubes in the boiling water. Turn to medium heat. While that is heating, melt the margarine (or butter) in a skillet. Add onions and stir over medium heat until thoroughly heated. Add onions and butter to the bouillon. Cook together about 30 minutes over medium heat, stirring often. Ladle into soup bowls, sprinkle croutons and top with cheese. Serve hot.

CROCK POT CHEESE SOUP

Utensils:

> crock pot
> knife
> stirring spoon
> measuring cup
> measuring spoon

Ingredients:

> 2 cans cream of celery soup or cream of
>   chicken soup
> 1 onion, chopped
> 1 pound sharp cheddar cheese, cubed
> 1 cup milk
> 1 cup water
> 1 teaspoon salt
> 1 teaspoon pepper

Put all ingredients in crock pot and cover. Cook on low heat for 4-5 hours. Stir occasionally.

CROCK POT POTATO SOUP

Utensils:

>crock pot (4-quart)
>knife
>stirring spoon
>measuring spoon and cup

Ingredients:

>6 potatoes, chopped
>1 large onion, chopped
>4 stalks celery, chopped
>2 teaspoons salt
>2 teaspoons pepper
>4 tablespoons margarine
>1 quart milk

Chop potatoes, onion and celery. Put all ingredients in crock pot. Cover and cook on low for 5-6 hours.

CREATE-A-SOUP

Soups are fun to make because you really can't go wrong. Be as creative as you want, using the ingredients you like — or as many leftover vegetables and meats as you find in the refrigerator. Have fun discovering your own favorite combinations.

Utensils:
>   soup pot
>   knife
>   spoon

Basic ingredients:
>   soup bone (or leftover meat or ground beef)
>   2 cans tomato sauce
>   salt and pepper to taste
>   water to cover bone or meat
>   1 medium onion, chopped

Choose from these (leftovers, canned or fresh):

corn	mixed vegetables
peas, green	potatoes (3 medium)
green beans	celery
carrots	cabbage

Put your soup bone (or other meat) in the pot, cover with water and bring to a boil. Turn the burner to medium heat. Add tomato sauce, onion, salt and pepper, and the assorted vegetables. Stir to mix. Cook at medium heat, stirring occasionally, about 30 minutes. Then turn heat to low and cook 3-4 hours so that flavors blend thoroughly — and deliciously!

Try your own combinations . . . You'll agree SOUP-MAKING is SOUP-ER!!

CASSEROLES
AND SIDE DISHES

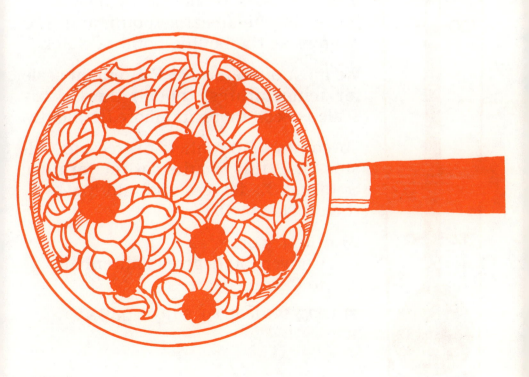

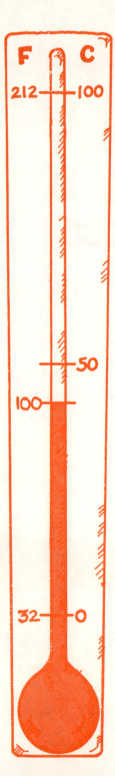

KID-BITS

FAHRENHEIT

Fahr en heit   (fer´an hīt) adj.

Fahrenheit — named for Gabriel Daniel Fahrenheit, a physicist who devised the scale — designates 32 degrees as the freezing point and 212 degrees as the boiling point of water.

CELSIUS

Cel si us   (sel´sē as) adj.

Celsius — named after Anders Celsius, a Swedish astronomer—designates 0 degrees as the freezing point and 100 degrees as the boiling point of water.

We most often use the Fahrenheit scale for temperatures, though the Celsius scale is seen more and more frequently.

To convert Fahrenheit degrees to Celsius, use this mathematical formula: Subtract 32 degrees and multiply by 5, then divide by 9.

Want to try one?
Convert 50 degrees Fahrenheit to Celsius degrees.

ANSWER: It's 10 degrees Celsius.

TUNA-NOODLE CASSEROLE

Utensils:

> pot
> baking dish
> can opener
> spoon

Ingredients:

> 1 small can of tuna
> 1 package macaroni and cheese
> ½ cup butter or margarine
> 1 can cream of mushroom soup
> ½ cup milk

Cook macaroni according to package directions. Drain. Put into greased baking dish. Add packaged cheese, butter or margarine, the soup and milk. Mix thoroughly. Bake for 30 minutes at 350 degrees.

Serves four.

SPAGHETTI CASSEROLE

Utensils:

    skillet
    fork
    paring knife
    baking dish
    can opener

Ingredients:

    1 pound ground beef
    1 small onion
    1 8-ounce package noodles (any variety)
    2 cans tomato soup
    1 package mozzarella cheese, shredded
    salt and pepper

Brown ground beef in skillet, stirring with fork to break it up. Peel and dice the onion. Add it to the ground beef; stir. Cook about 5 minutes more. Pour off excess fat CAREFULLY. Set aside.

Cook noodles according to package directions. Drain.

Put noodles, ground beef and onion and the two cans of tomato soup into the baking dish. Mix well.

Bake for 15 minutes at 350 degrees. Remove from oven and sprinkle shredded mozzarella cheese over the top of the casserole. Return it to oven and heat until cheese is thoroughly melted. Serve hot. Serves four.

CHILI CASSEROLE

Utensils:

      large skillet
      fork
      1½-quart casserole baking dish, greased
      measuring cup

Ingredients:

      2 tablespoons oil
      1 pound ground beef
      ½ cup chopped onions
      1 15-ounce can chili con carne
          (with beans)
      salt and pepper
      2 cups nacho cheese corn chips
          (slightly crushed)
      1 cup cheddar cheese, grated

Heat oil in large skillet. Add ground beef, breaking it apart with a fork. When it is browned, add the onions and cook about 5 minutes.

Remove from heat and carefully drain off the excess fat. Stir in the chili, salt and pepper (to taste).

Place a layer of broken corn chips (1½ cups) in the bottom of a greased baking dish. Cover with the meat mixture, then sprinkle on the cheese.

Bake at 350 degrees for 20 minutes. Remove from the oven and sprinkle on the remaining ½ cup of corn chips. Serve.

Serves six.

BUSY DAY CASSEROLE

Utensils:
>2-quart sauce pan with lid
>2-quart casserole
>measuring cup
>mixing bowl

Ingredients:
>1 can cream of mushroom soup
>1 soup can full of milk
>½ green pepper, chopped
>1 8-ounce package noodles,
>   cooked and drained
>2 cups (8 ounces) shredded Swiss cheese

Stir soup, milk and green pepper together. Mix well. This works best if you stir in a little milk, then a little soup, instead of dumping it all together. Grease the casserole dish with a small amount of margarine. Put half the noodles, cheese, and sauce in the dish in layers. Repeat with the remaining ingredients. Bake at 350 degrees for 35 minutes. Serves 4-6.

Add bits of ham or another favorite meat if you want to vary the casserole. Put the meat in as another layer.

QUICK BEEF BAKE

Utensils:

      skillet
      knife
      spatula
      spoon
      2-quart pan and lid
      can opener
      measuring cup
      casserole dish

Ingredients:

      1 pound ground beef
      2 tablespoons onion, chopped
      1 can cream of mushroom soup
      ½ cup milk
      1 package macaroni and cheese dinner
      2 tablespoons margarine

Brown the ground beef and onion in a skillet. Drain off excess fat CAREFULLY. Boil the macaroni according to package directions. Drain well. Mix macaroni and cheese, milk and margarine. Put this mixture, the mushroom soup and the ground beef mixture in a casserole dish. Bake for 20 minutes at 350 degrees.

FRITO SPECIAL

Utensils:
>skillet
>spatula
>knife
>cutting board
>small bowls

Ingredients:
>1 pound ground beef
>1 small onion, chopped
>1 can chili beans
>1 10-ounce can enchilada sauce
>1 5-ounce can tomato sauce
>1 package Fritos
>1 4-ounce package grated cheese
>shredded lettuce
>chopped tomatoes
>sour cream

Brown ground beef and onion. Drain fat CAREFULLY. Add beans, enchilada sauce, and simmer for one hour. To serve: put Fritos on plate first, then meat sauce, then onion, lettuce, cheese, tomatoes and sour cream. Yield: 4-6 servings.

BURGER AND FRIES

Utensils:
>skillet
>casserole dish
>spatula
>spoon
>can opener

Ingredients:
>1 pound ground beef
>3 cups frozen french fries
>1 can cream of mushroom soup

Brown ground beef in skillet and drain off excess fat CAREFULLY. Put drained meat in the casserole dish. Open the can of soup and mix it with the ground beef. Put frozen fries on top. Bake in 350 degree oven for 30 minutes. Serves 4.

FANCY FRIES

Utensils:

    cookie sheet
    measuring cup
    measuring spoons

Ingredients:

    3 cups frozen french fries
    ½ teaspoon salt
    ½ cup grated cheddar cheese or
        Parmesan cheese
    small amount of margarine to grease
        cookie sheet

Put frozen potatoes on lightly greased cookie sheet. Sprinkle with salt. Bake uncovered, 450 degrees for 15 minutes. Remove potatoes from the oven and sprinkle with your choice of cheese, then bake 2 minutes longer or until cheese is melted. Yields: 3 servings.

ROSY RICE

Utensils:

      measuring cup
      large spoon
      saucepan with lid
      measuring spoons
      paring knife

Ingredients:

      1 cup rice (quick cook)
      ¼ cup chopped onion
      3 tablespoons margarine
      ½ cup tomato sauce
      1½ cups water
      ½ teaspoon salt
      ¼ teaspoon pepper

Measure 1 cup rice, ¼ cup onion. Brown in 3 table-spoons of butter in the saucepan. Add and stir 1½ cups water, ½ cup tomato sauce, and salt and pepper. Cover and simmer 25-30 minutes.

CREAMY NOODLES

Utensils:

>saucepan
>mixing spoon
>measuring cup

Ingredients:

>1 8-ounce package noodles
>½ cup melted butter
>½ cup grated Parmesan cheese
>¼ cup milk, room temperature, or cream
>salt and pepper

Prepare noodles according to package directions. Drain. Toss with butter, cheese and cream until well coated. Season to taste with salt and pepper.

SCRUMPTIOUS SWEETS

KID-BITS

CALORIE   cal-o-rie   (kal´ə rē) n.

A calorie is a unit used for measuring the energy produced by food when it is oxidized in the body.

If we were trying to lose weight, we would carefully count the calories in the food we eat so that we would take in fewer calories than our bodies would use up. Which of the following foods would we likely avoid if we were carefully watching our calories?

Pecan pie, 1 slice   Cucumber, 6-8 slices

Peanuts, 1 cup   Orange, fresh

ANSWER: Probably, we would pass up the peanuts (840 calories) and the pecan pie (495 calories) in favor of the cucumbers (5) and the fresh orange (65).

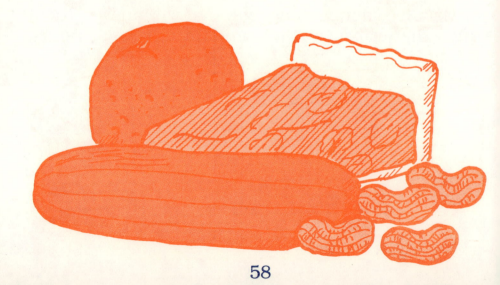

58

SINK OR SWIM

Utensils:
- mixing bowl
- 1 cup measure
- mixing spoon

Ingredients:
- 1 package (3-ounce) strawberry gelatin
- 1 cup boiling water
- 1 cup cold water or ginger ale
- 1 cup fruit combinations*

***FRUITS THAT SINK:** Mandarin oranges, seedless grapes, drained canned fruits (packed in heavy syrup) such as peach slices, sliced pear halves, crushed pineapple or pineapple chunks, cherries or apricots.

****FRUITS THAT SWIM:** Banana slices, apple wedges or diced apple, strawberry halves, fresh orange sections, fresh sliced peaches or pears, marshmallows or coarsely chopped nuts.

Dissolve gelatin in boiling water in heatproof glass bowl. Add cold water. Add fruit that will sink, then add fruits that will swim. Chill until firm, at least 3 hours.

BERRY GOOD SUNDAE

Utensils:
  fork
  dessert dish
  spoon

Ingredients:
  fresh strawberries
  cookies
  ice cream
  whipped cream

Mash some fresh strawberries with a fork. Crumble a few of your favorite cookies into another dish with your hand.

Put layers of ice cream, cookies and mashed strawberries in a tall, clear glass. Top it with whipped cream, ice cream and a fresh strawberry. Watch your friends smile!

DIP-IT-E-DO

Utensils:
>   knife
>   toothpicks
>   sauce pan

Ingredients:
>   4 bananas
>   1 6-ounce package semi-sweet chocolate chips
>   ½ cup chopped peanuts

Peel the bananas. Cut them in fourths (four equal pieces). Put toothpicks through banana pieces.

Melt in pan over low heat the package of chocolate chips. (Watch carefully. It will stick easily.) Dip banana into chocolate, then roll in chopped peanuts. YUMMY!

ERIC'S
BIG BIRD COOKIES

Utensils:

mixing bowl
mixing spoon
measuring cup
cookie cutter
cookie sheet

Ingredients:

¾ cup softened margarine
1 cup sugar
2 eggs
1 teaspoon vanilla
2½ cups flour
1 teaspoon baking powder
1 teaspoon salt
sugar (about a cup)
food coloring

Mix first seven ingredients. Refrigerate for 1 hour. Roll out and cut 32 big cookies. Mix sugar with food coloring and pat on top of cookies before baking. Bake in 400 degree oven for 8 minutes on ungreased cookie sheet. Yields 32 cookies.

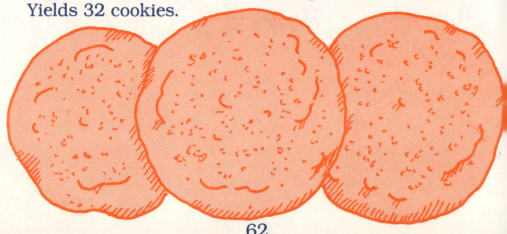

PUPPET SUGAR COOKIES

Utensils:

mixing bowl
measuring cup
teaspoon measure
mixing spoon
cookie cutter
knife
wooden sticks
foil
cookie sheet

Ingredients:

1½ cup melted margarine
2 cups sugar
2 eggs
2 teaspoons vanilla
5 cups flour
2 teaspoons baking powder
1 teaspoon salt

Combine butter, sugar, eggs, and vanilla. Sift together flour, baking powder and salt. Combine sifted ingredients with butter mixture. Chill 1 hour.

Roll out dough. Use cookie cutter or cut designs with a knife. Insert stick in lower middle end of cookie. Place on foil and bake on ungreased cookie sheet in 400 degree oven 8-10 minutes.

JAKE'S BROWNIE CHIP COOKIES

Utensils:
>mixing bowl
>mixing spoons
>measuring cup
>cookie sheet

Ingredients:
>1 package brownie mix
>2 eggs
>¼ cup oil
>1 cup semi-sweet chocolate chips

Preheat oven to 350 degrees. Grease cookie sheets. Combine brownie mix, eggs and oil. Beat. Stir in chips. Drop by spoonful 2-3 inches apart on cookie sheets. Bake 8-10 minutes.

Frost, if desired.

CHOCOLATE FROSTING: 1 box confectioners' sugar, ½ stick margarine (melted), 3 tablespoons cocoa, and small amount of milk for right consistency. (Be careful. A little milk will go a long way with confectioners' sugar. It's easy to overdo. Add a few drops at a time and stir; then add a few more drops.)

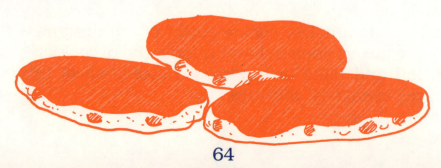

JAYMEE'S ENERGY BIRTHDAY COOKIES

Utensils:

mixing bowl
mixing spoon
sifter
cookie sheet

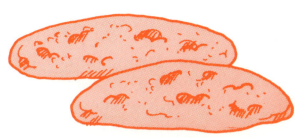

Ingredients:

½ cup butter
½ cup brown sugar
½ cup white sugar
1 egg (well beaten)
1 teaspoon vanilla
1 cup flour
½ teaspoon baking soda
¼ teaspoon cinnamon
¼ teaspoon salt
¼ teaspoon baking powder
1 cup dry oatmeal
1 cup cornflakes
½ cup raisins
½ cup chopped pecans

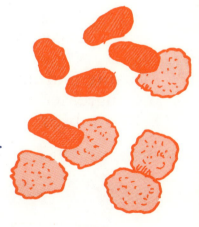

Cream butter, add sugars, then egg and vanilla. Sift dry ingredients together and add to creamed mixture. Add cornflakes, oatmeal, raisins and pecans. Roll into small balls and place about 2 inches apart on greased cookie sheet. Bake at 350 degrees 10-15 minutes.

1-2-3-4 PEANUT BUTTER COOKIES

Utensils:
- mixing bowl
- mixing spoon
- measuring cup
- measuring spoons
- cookie sheet

Ingredients:
- 2 cups peanut butter
- 2 cups white sugar
- 2 eggs
- 2 teaspoons vanilla

Measure and mix four ingredients. Drop by teaspoon on ungreased cookie sheet. Bake at 325 degrees for 8-10 minutes.

JOEY'S CHOCOLATE CHIP COOKIES

Utensils:

      electric mixer
      mixing bowl
      mixing spoon
      measuring cups
      measuring spoons
      cookie sheets
      flour sifter

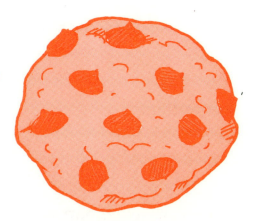

Ingredients:

      2½ cups flour
      1 teaspoon salt
      1 cup margarine, softened
      1 cup brown sugar, packed
      2/3 cup granulated sugar
      2 eggs
      1 teaspoon vanilla
      1 tablespoon hot water
      1 teaspoon baking soda
      1 12-ounce package chocolate chips

Sift flour and salt. Cream margarine and brown and white sugars on medium speed of electric mixer. Add eggs and vanilla; beat on medium speed. Dissolve soda in the tablespoon of hot water. Add to batter. Add sifted flour and salt to batter; mix. Stir in chocolate chips. Beat about 1½ minutes. Drop by half teaspoons on greased cookie sheet. Bake at 350 degrees for 8-10 minutes. Yield: 6 dozen.

OATMEAL FUDGE COOKIES

Utensils:
> measuring cups
> mixing bowl
> mixing spoon
> pot
> waxed paper

Ingredients:
> 2 cups sugar
> ½ cup cocoa
> ½ cup milk
> ½ cup margarine
> 1 teaspoon vanilla
> 3 cups instant or regular oatmeal,
>   uncooked

Mix together sugar, cocoa and milk. Bring to a boil. Add margarine and stir until melted. Boil 2 minutes. Remove from heat. Add vanilla and oatmeal. Stir and drop onto waxed paper by tablespoonfuls. Cool.

SPECIAL OATMEAL COOKIES

Utensils:

>sauce pan
>mixing spoons
>measuring cup
>measuring spoons
>medium sized mixing bowl

Ingredients:

>1 stick butter or margarine
>½ cup milk
>2 cups sugar
>¼ cup cocoa
>1 teaspoon vanilla
>¼ to ½ cup peanut butter
>3 cups oatmeal, uncooked

Put butter, milk and sugar in sauce pan. Bring to boil and boil about 5 minutes. Add cocoa. Pour into medium-sized mixing bowl with oats and peanut butter. Add vanilla. Mix, let cook for a minute. Drop by spoonfuls on waxed paper and cool.

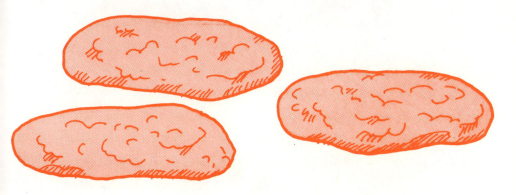

GINGERBREAD MEN

Utensils:

> tablespoon measure
> cookie cutter
> large mixing bowl
> wooden spoon
> pastry cloth
> sifter
> rolling pin
> cookie sheet

Ingredients:

> 1 box gingerbread mix
> 3 rounded tablespoons powdered sugar
> 4 tablespoons orange or lemon juice
> shortening or cooking oil
> flour

Sift gingerbread mix and sugar into mixing bowl. Add the juice and stir until moist. Form into a ball and roll out on floured pastry cloth to ⅛-inch thickness. Cut with floured gingerbread man cutter. Place on a greased cookie sheet and bake at 350 degrees 10-12 minutes.

PEANUT BUTTER BALLS

Utensils:

measuring cup
teaspoon measure
mixing bowl
mixing spoon
baking sheet

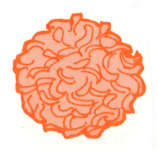

Ingredients:

1 cup peanut butter
1 cup powdered sugar
2 teaspoons butter
½ teaspoon vanilla
2½ cups Rice Krispies
1 cup grated coconut

Mix all ingredients together in a bowl, except the coconut. Shape the dough into balls. Roll the balls in the coconut. Chill on baking sheets until firm.

Store in covered container.

Makes 3 dozen balls.

PEANUT BUTTER, HONEY PUFF

Utensils:

     measuring cup
     measuring spoon
     mixing spoon
     waxed paper

Ingredients:

     ½ cup peanut butter
     ½ cup nonfat dry milk
     ½ cup honey
     ½ teaspoon vanilla
     ¼ cup crushed cornflakes

Mix the first four ingredients together. Roll into small balls. Roll the balls in crushed cornflakes. Put balls on waxed paper. Chill one hour and serve.

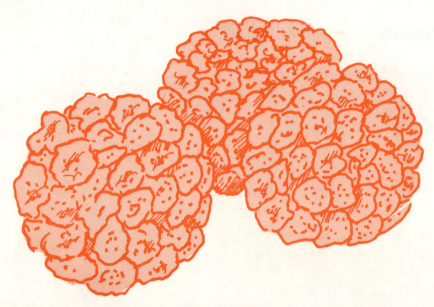

CHINESE CRISPIES

Utensils:

      sauce pan
      large spoon
      waxed paper
      measuring cup
      teaspoons

Ingredients:

      ½ cup white syrup
      ½ cup sugar
      1 cup peanut butter
      1 cup chow mein noodles

Measure sugar and syrup into sauce pan. Stir and bring to a boil. Measure peanut butter and chow mein noodles. Take pan off stove and stir these into syrup mixture.

Drop by spoon on wax paper. Cool.

NO BAKE NUGGETS

Utensils:

measuring cup
rolling pin
teaspoon
waxed paper
sauce pan
wooden spoon

Ingredients:

1 stick margarine
1 cup sugar
½ cup condensed milk
10 large marshmallows
1 cup crushed graham crackers
1 cup chopped nuts

Combine margarine, sugar, and milk; cool for six minutes, stirring constantly. Stir in remaining ingredients. Drop in small balls onto waxed paper.

QUICK AND EASY BROWNIES

Utensils:

>mixing bowl
>measuring cup
>mixing spoon
>9 x 13 inch baking pan

Ingredients:

>Family size package of brownie mix
>>(the product with the liquid
>>chocolate works best)
>
>4 eggs
>¼ cup water
>1 cup dairy sour cream
>1 12-ounce package of milk chocolate chips

Mix brownie mix, eggs and water until all ingredients are moistened. Stir in sour cream. Stir in chocolate chips. Spread into greased baking pan and bake at 350 degrees for 30 minutes.

Brownies may look undone, but this is what makes them soft and chewy.

Frost with chocolate frosting while still warm.

CHOCOLATE FROSTING

Utensils:
> small skillet
> mixing bowl
> measuring cups
> measuring spoons
> knife
> mixing spoon

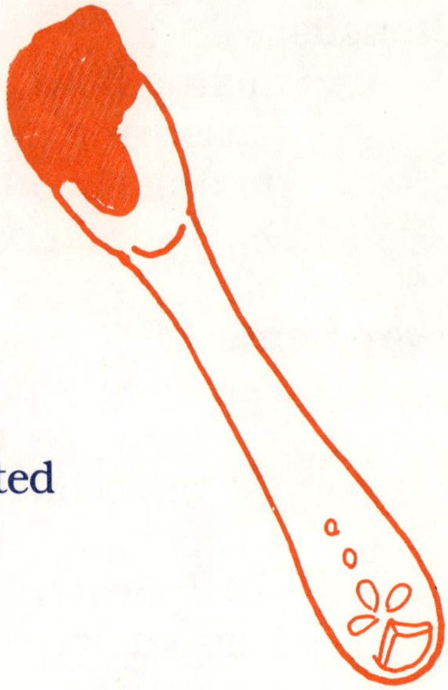

Ingredients:
> 1 stick margarine, melted
> 3 tablespoons of cocoa
> ¼ teaspoon salt
> 1 tablespoon milk
> 1 teaspoon vanilla

Melt margarine in skillet. Sift confectioner's sugar, cocoa, and salt together. Add vanilla, melted margarine, and milk; mix. (You may add more milk, a drop or two at a time, to get the consistency you want.)

PEANUT BUTTER CHOCOLATE BARS

Utensils:

      mixing bowl
      measuring cup
      mixing spoon
      flour sifter
      electric mixer
      double boiler
      rolling pin
      knife

Ingredients:

      1 1-pound box confectioners' sugar
      1 cup margarine, softened
      1½ cups crunchy peanut butter
      3 cups graham cracker crumbs
      1 6-ounce package chocolate chips

Sift confectioners' sugar into mixing bowl. Add peanut butter and butter. Beat with electric mixer about two minutes until light and creamy (medium speed). Crush graham crackers with rolling pin and stir into creamed mixture. Pat into 9 x 13 baking pan. Melt chocolate chips over hot water in double boiler. Spread chocolate over the peanut butter-graham cracker layer. Let stand until chocolate cools. Cut into small pieces. Yield: 60 pieces.

CHOCOLATE PIZZA

Utensils:

> flour sifter
> electric mixer
> 2 pie pans or 1 large pizza pan
> mixing bowl
> measuring cup and spoons
> mixing spoon
> small skillet to melt margarine

Ingredients:

> 2 cups flour
> 1 teaspoon salt
> 1 teaspoon baking powder
> 1/4 teaspoon baking soda
> 2/3 cup margarine, melted
> 2 cups brown sugar (firmly packed)
> 2 eggs
> 2 tablespoons hot water
> 2 teaspoons vanilla
> 1 cup chopped nuts
> 1 12-ounce package chocolate chips
> 2 cups miniature marshmallows

Sift flour, salt, baking powder, and soda. Mix melted margarine and brown sugar. Beat with an electric mixer at medium speed until well blended. Add eggs, beat, add hot water and vanilla and mix well. Add the dry ingredients 1/4 at a time, stirring well each time. Add nuts. If you are using the pie pans, divide dough in half or use all of it for a large pizza pan. Grease pan with small amount of margarine. Spread dough in pans. Sprinkle dough with the chocolate chips and marshmallows. Bake at 350 degrees for 25 minutes. Cool in pans and cut into wedges or squares.

JESSICA'S HAPPY FACES

Utensils:

12 foil pot pie pans (save them up)
measuring cup
spoon
mixing bowl
can opener

Ingredients:

20-ounce package chocolate cake mix
2 teaspoons butter
2 tablespoons brown sugar
raisins
12 pineapple rings

Prepare cake mix according to the directions on the package. Grease pot pie pans with shortening. Put a small amount of butter and sugar in the bottom of each pan. Put a pineapple ring on top of the butter and sugar. Place raisins in the ring, making "eyes," "nose," and "mouth." Next, spoon prepared cake mix over pineapple slices until the pan is about 2/3 full. Bake at 375 degrees for 30 minutes.

Cool thoroughly, then turn upside down onto a plate and carefully remove the pan. Yields 12 small "happy faces."

CRAZY CAKE

Utensils:

    cake pan
    sifter
    mixing spoon
    measuring cup

Ingredients:

    1½ cups flour (sifted)
    1 cup sugar
    1 teaspoon baking soda
    ½ teaspoon salt
    3 tablespoons cocoa

Sift these ingredients into a flat ungreased cake pan. Make three indentations in mixture. In each indentation, place one of the following:

    1 teaspoon vanilla
    1 teaspoon vinegar
    5 tablespoons oil or shortening

Over whole mixture pour 1 cup cold water. Mix in pan until smooth. Bake at 350 degrees for 35 minutes. Remove from oven. Let cool 10 minutes and turn upside down on rack. After cooling, frost. (Cake can be left in pan for cooling and frosting, if you prefer.)

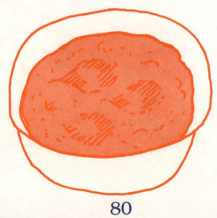

RUSSIAN COFFEE CAKE

Utensils:

>mixing bowl
>measuring cup
>mixing spoon
>8-inch round cake pan
>knife

Ingredients:

>2½ cups flour
>1½ cups brown sugar
>½ cup butter or margarine (softened)
>1 teaspoon cinnamon
>1 cup sour milk or buttermilk
>1 teaspoon baking soda

Mix together flour, brown sugar, butter and cinnamon. Cut butter into the dry ingredients with a knife until it looks like soft crumbs. Reserve one cup of the dry mixture. Stir baking soda into milk and add to crumb mixture. Mix well. Put into greased and floured round cake pan. Cover with the cup of dry mixture.

Bake at 350 degrees for 30-45 minutes. Serves 6-8.

TORY'S SURPRISE CUPCAKES

Utensils:

    cupcake pans
    48 cupcake papers
    measuring cups
    spoon
    mixing bowl

Ingredients:

    20-ounce package yellow cake mix
    16 ounces softened cream cheese
    2 eggs, beaten
    1 teaspoon salt
    2/3 cup sugar
    12-ounce package chocolate chips

Prepare cake mix according to the directions on the package. Fill cups 1/3 full with this batter. Combine cream cheese, eggs, salt, sugar and chocolate chips. Drop this mixture by teaspoons into each cup of batter. Bake at 350 degrees for 30 minutes. 4 dozen.

PARTY CONE CUPCAKES

Utensils:
- flour sifter
- electric mixer
- mixing bowl
- measuring spoons and cups
- cookie sheet

Ingredients:
- 1¼ cup all-purpose flour
- 1½ teaspoon baking powder
- ½ teaspoon salt
- 1/3 cup butter or margarine (softened)
- 1 cup granulated sugar
- 1 egg
- ¾ cup milk
- 1 teaspoon vanilla
- flat-bottom ice cream cones

Sift flour, baking powder, and salt together. Cream sugar and butter with electric mixer; add egg and beat. Add vanilla. Beat in flour and milk, alternately until well blended. Beat two minutes.

Place ice cream cones on baking sheet. Spoon batter to half-fill each cone. Bake at 375 degrees for 15-20 minutes or until a toothpick inserted in the center of the cake comes out clean. Transfer to a wire rack to cool.

Frost with your favorite frosting.

NANA'S
BANANA CANDY

Utensils:
  mixing bowl
  mixing spoon
  rolling pin
  measuring cup

Ingredients:
  1 box confectioners' sugar
  1 small-medium banana
  peanut butter (crunchy or plain)

Pour confectioners' sugar into mixing bowl. Reserve ½ cup. Peel banana and mash it up (use your hands!) into the sugar. Mix well. It will form a dough. Sprinkle the confectioners' sugar you reserved onto your countertop; spread it around. Place your dough on it and roll it out flat with the rolling pin — about ½ inch thick. Now, spread peanut butter on the dough to the thickness you like. Then, starting at one edge, begin rolling up the dough (like a jelly roll). Place the banana roll in the refrigerator for about 1 hour. Slice and serve.

EASY PEANUT BUTTER CANDY

Utensils:

    1 large knife
    chopping board
    mixing bowl
    large spoon
    measuring cup
    cellophane wrap

Ingredients:

    1/3 cup honey
    1/3 cup peanut butter
    ¼ cup toasted wheat germ
    ½ cup dry milk
    ¼ cup chopped peanuts

Combine honey and peanut butter and cream until smooth. Add the toasted wheat germ and mix thoroughly. Dump the peanuts into the bowl and work them into the candy thoroughly with your fingers. Roll the candy into a log shape about ¾ inch thick. Use your hands. Do it gently or the candy will stick to the board — and to you! Cut the candy roll into 1-inch pieces and wrap each one in cellophane wrap. Store it in a covered container. If you like it chewy, store it in the refrigerator.

NO COOK FUDGE

Utensils:

1 large mixing bowl
1 large spoon for mixing
1 9 x 15 inch baking pan
measuring cup
1 small, sharp knife
cellophane wrap

Ingredients:

1 cup dry, nonfat milk powder
1 cup peanut butter or carob powder
1 cup chopped walnuts
1 cup sunflower seeds
1 cup sesame seeds
1 cup oats
½ cup honey
½ cup water
butter or margarine for greasing pan

Grease the baking pan and set it aside. Put the milk powder, peanut butter or carob powder, honey, oats and water into the mixing bowl. Blend together well. Add the chopped walnuts. Mix well until all ingredients are blended and are sticking together. Spoon the fudge into the greased baking pan and press it down so that it covers the entire pan. Cut it into squares and wrap each one individually. Store in a covered container — or in the refrigerator if you like chewy candy.

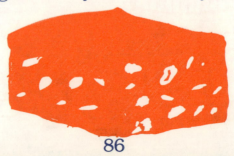

GO NUTTY SNACK

Utensils:

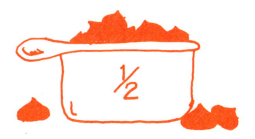

    plastic bag
    mixing bowls (2)
    wooden spoon
    measuring cup
    cookie sheet

Ingredients:

    8 double graham crackers
    ¼ cup honey
    1 cup chunky peanut butter
    ½ cup chocolate chips
    ½ cup instant dry milk

Put the graham crackers in a plastic bag, twist shut and pound with your fist to make a lot of crumbs. Pour crumbs into a bowl. Mix the remaining ingredients together in another bowl with a wooden spoon. Shape the mixture into little balls and roll them in the graham cracker crumbs. Put your snacks on a cookie sheet and chill.

VARIATIONS: Try rolling your mixture in ground peanuts, coconut, cereal crumbs, granola.

ENERGY CANDY

Utensils:

- measuring cup
- mixing bowl
- mixing spoon
- knife
- waxed paper

Ingredients:

- 1 cup honey
- 1 cup peanut butter
- 2 cups non-fat dry milk
- 2 cups raisins
- 1 cup chopped nuts
- 2 cups uncooked oatmeal

Mix honey and peanut butter in bowl. Gradually add dry milk, mixing well. Mix in raisins, nuts and oatmeal. Shape into log; wrap with waxed paper. Chill until firm.

To serve, cut into one-inch slices. Keep refrigerated.

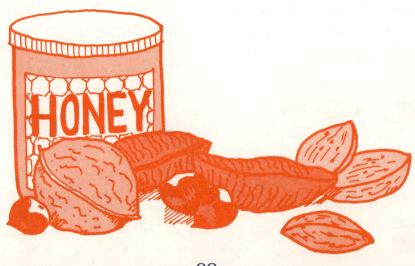

MIXED FRUIT CANDY BALLS

Utensils:
3 small baking pans for toasting nuts
1 large knife
1 chopping board
blender or food grinder (optional)
1 large mixing bowl
large mixing spoon
measuring cup and spoons

Ingredients:
½ cup raisins
½ cup pitted dates
½ cup figs
½ cup pitted prunes
½ cup chopped nuts

1 orange, peeled and seeded
1/3 cup wheat germ
½ teaspoon cinnamon
¼ cup sesame seeds
¼ cup almonds, sliced

Preheat oven to 350 degrees. Put the sliced almonds in one small baking pan, the sesame seeds in another and the wheat germ in the third (if your wheat germ is raw. If it is toasted, do not roast again.). Place the pans in the oven and bake until the nuts, seeds, and wheat germ are light brown (10 to 15 minutes). Remove and cool. Chop the raisins, dates, figs, prunes, and orange slices into very, very tiny pieces. If you use a blender, put them in the blender and blend with cover on for about a minute. If using a food grinder, simply put these ingredients through the grinder. When the ingredients are finely chopped, put them in a large mixing bowl. Add the wheat germ and cinnamon and mix together thoroughly. With your hands, shape 36 tightly packed candy balls from the mixture. Roll half the balls in sesame seeds and half in toasted almonds.

Refrigerate until you are ready to serve.

CHOCOLATE FLING

Utensils:

>small mixing bowl
>hand beater
>2-cup measuring cup
>1-cup measuring cup
>rubber scraper
>spoon
>6 dessert glasses

>1 package (4-serving size) instant
>   chocolate pudding
>2 cups milk
>1 cup thawed non-dairy whipped topping

Prepare pudding mix with milk as directed on package. Let stand for 5 minutes.

Fold whipped topping into pudding, creating a marbled effect.

Spoon into dessert glasses. Chill until ready to serve.

Makes about 3 cups or 6 servings.

AMBROSIA PUDDING

Utensils:
>   hand beater
>   small mixing bowl
>   strainer
>   mixing spoon
>   1 cup liquid measure
>   grater
>   measuring spoons
>   dessert glasses or bowl

Ingredients:
>   1 package (4-serving size)
>   coconut cream instant pudding
>   2 cups milk
>   1 can (11-ounce) mandarin orange sections,
>   drained
>   ½ teaspoon grated orange rind
>   (optional)

Prepare pudding mix with milk as directed on package. Fold in orange sections and orange rind, reserving a few sections for garnish, if desired. Pour into individual dessert glasses or a serving bowl and chill. Garnish with reserved sections and mint sprigs, if desired. Makes about 2½ cups or 5 servings.

FROZEN POPS

Utensils:

2-cup liquid measure
small mixing bowl
hand beater
rubber scraper
six 5-ounce paper cups
6 wooden sticks or plastic spoons
foil or wax paper

Ingredients:
1 package (4-serving size) instant pudding,
    any flavor
2 cups milk

Prepare pudding mix with milk as directed on package. Pour into the paper cups. Insert wooden stick or plastic spoon into each cup for a handle. Press a square of aluminum foil or wax paper down onto pudding to cover, piercing center of foil square with handle.

Freeze until firm, at least 5 hours.

Press firmly on bottom of cup to release pop. Serve plain or dip in melted chocolate and sprinkles. Makes 6 pops.

MELTED CHOCOLATE: Combine ½ cup chocolate-flavored chips and 2 tablespoons of water in a sauce pan and cook and stir until melted and smooth.

BEST BREADS

KID-BITS

CARBOHYDRATE Car bo hy drate (kär'bə hī'drāt) n.

Carbohydrates form an important class of foods, supplying energy to the body.

Which of the following foods would you choose if you were looking for a high-energy food (one with the most carbohydrates)?

> Raisins, 1 cup
>
> Chicken, 6 ounces, broiled
>
> Sherbet, 1 cup
>
> Chocolate milkshake, 10 ounce

ANSWER: Raisins, 1 cup, with 112 grams of carbohydrates. The chicken has ZERO grams, the sherbet, 59, and the milkshake, 63.

94

CHOCOLATE CHIP FRUIT BREAD

Utensils:

      mixing bowl
      mixing spoon
      sifter
      loaf pan

Ingredients:

      1 cup butter
      1 cup sugar
      2 eggs
      2 cups flour
      1 teaspoon soda
      1 cup mashed banana (about 2)
      ¼ cup chopped maraschino cherries
      ¼ cup chocolate chips
      ¼ cup nut pieces

Cream butter, sugar, and add eggs. Beat well. Sift flour and soda. Mash bananas with a fork. Add bananas and flour mixture alternately to egg mixture. Mix in remaining ingredients. Pour into greased loaf pan. Bake at 350 degrees for 1 hour. Makes 1 large loaf.

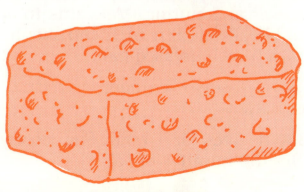

APPLESAUCE NUT BREAD

Utensils:

mixing bowl
measuring cup
measuring spoons
sifter
large mixing spoon
9 x 5 inch baking pan

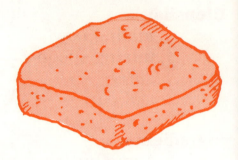

Ingredients:

1 cup sugar
1 cup applesauce
1/3 cup oil
2 eggs
3 tablespoons milk
2 cups flour

1 teaspoon baking soda
½ teaspoon baking powder
½ teaspoon cinnamon
⅛ teaspoon salt
¼ teaspoon nutmeg
¾ cup chopped pecans

Topping:

¼ cup brown sugar
½ teaspoon cinnamon
¼ cup chopped pecans

In a large mixing bowl, combine sugar, applesauce, oil, eggs and milk. Sift together flour, soda, baking powder, cinnamon, salt and nutmeg. Add this to applesauce mixture and beat well. Stir in ¾ cup chopped pecans. Turn into 9 x 5 inch greased pan.

Combine brown sugar, cinnamon, pecans. Sprinkle evenly over batter.

Bake at 350 degrees for 1 hour. Cap loosely with foil after the first 30 minutes of baking.

LOGAN BREAD

Utensils:

measuring cup
measuring spoons
large, greased pan
mixing spoon

Ingredients:

1 tablespoon baking powder
1 cup raw sugar
5 pounds whole grain flour
 (any kind, any mixture)
2 cups powdered milk (dry)
1 pound raisins (more if desired)
1 pound dried peaches and/or other fruits
 (chopped)
1 pound chopped almonds
 (or more, if desired)

Grease your hands and mix these ingredients together. Then, add and mix thoroughly:

2 cups molasses   ¼ cup peanut oil
1 pound honey   4 cups water

Place dough in large, greased pan; it should be about 1 inch deep. Bake it for two hours in a 300 degree oven. Cut in 2½ x 2½ inch squares, stand on edge and dry in low oven.

This is a high calorie, high energy bread that's great for active kids. It can be used on short outings and will keep for a long time. Drying can be eliminated and squares can be wrapped in plastic wrap and frozen. If dried, store in a dry place. This is an historic bread — used by early settlers. It keeps indefinitely without refrigeration.

97

BURP BREAD

Utensils:

    measuring cup
    measuring spoons
    mixing bowl (large, with lid)
    greased baking pans

Ingredients:

    9 cups flour
    2 packages yeast
    4 eggs
    1½ cups water
    1 tablespoon salt
    1½ cups scalded milk
    1 cup melted butter
    2/3 cup sugar

Put all of flour in a large bowl. Make a "well" in the center. Add part of hot milk to water and dissolve yeast in it. Add rest of milk, eggs, salt and sugar; mix well. Pour this mixture into center of flour. Do not stir! Seal or cover bowl until seal pops up — yes, it burps! — 1½ hours. Add melted butter and stir well. Reseal bowl and leave until seal pops up again — about 1½ hours. Turn out onto well-floured surface and cut into dinner rolls. Bake in well-greased pans at 350 degrees for 20-30 minutes. Makes 3 large pans of rolls.

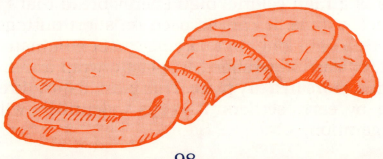

PITA BREAD

Pita is a flat, round bread that is Middle Eastern in origin. Its two sides form a pocket which can be stuffed with various foods — salads, fillings, luncheon meats, whatever you like.

Utensils:
    measuring cup
    measuring spoon
    mixing bowl
    mixing spoon
    cloth
    baking sheets

Ingredients:
    2 packages dry yeast
    ½ teaspoon sugar
    2 cups warm water
    ½ cup oil
    1 tablespoon salt
    6 cups unbleached all-purpose flour
    oil to grease bowl
    cornmeal to spread on baking sheet

Dissolve yeast, sugar, ½ cup warm water in bowl. Let stand for 10 minutes. Add 1½ cups water, oil, salt and flour gradually. Mix these ingredients thoroughly.

Put dough on lightly floured flat surface and knead about 10 minutes until smooth and elastic. Form into ball. Grease large bowl and put dough into bowl, turn over so it is completely covered with oil. Cover with cloth. Let rise about 2 hours until doubled in bulk. Keep in warm place. Punch down dough. Divide into 9 balls. Let rise about ½ hour. Sprinkle corn meal on baking sheets. Preheat oven to 500 degrees. Roll each ball into a circle on a lightly floured surface. Put circles on baking sheets. Place baking sheet with pita on lowest rack in oven for 5 minutes. It will puff up like a small balloon when it is in the oven, but it deflates as it cools. Transfer baking sheet to the highest rack for 2-3 minutes. Remove from oven and cool thoroughly on rack. Serve stuffed with desired filling. To store, wrap in plastic as soon as it is cooled. Makes 8-9 loaves.

MONKEY ROLLS

Utensils:
>   measuring cup
>   measuring spoons
>   plastic bag
>   tube baking pan
>   mixing spoon

Ingredients:
>   2 cans biscuits
>   ½ cup chopped nuts
>   1 stick melted margarine
>   3 tablespoons water
>   1 cup sugar
>   2 teaspoons cinnamon

Cut biscuits in half. Drop them in a bag with the cinnamon and sugar. Shake till well coated. Place in tube pan; sprinkle with nuts.

Make mixture of leftover sugar and cinnamon by adding water and melted butter. Stir. Place rolls in 300-degree oven till raised and light brown. Pour the sugar liquid over them and return to 350 degrees for about 20 minutes.

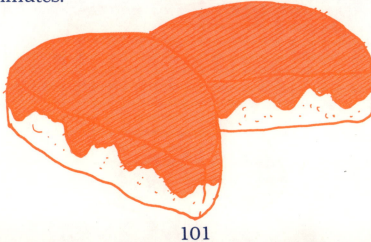

DOUGH BEARS

Utensils:

    cookie sheet
    rolling pin
    pastry brush
    pastry board

Ingredients:

    1 loaf frozen bread dough
    1 egg white

Defrost the bread dough. Roll dough in a ball, then pat it out. Pinch off pieces for the body, legs, arms, head and ears of a bear. Put your bear together, brushing the parts with egg white to help them stick together. Let the bread bear rise in a warm place until double in size. Then brush the whole bear with egg white. Bake at 350 degrees until golden brown, about 20-30 minutes.

CINNAMON TOAST

Utensils:

      broiler
      knife

Ingredients:

      2 slices bread
      margarine
      sugar
      cinnamon

Spread margarine onto bread. Sprinkle sugar and cinnamon onto bread. Toast under broiler.

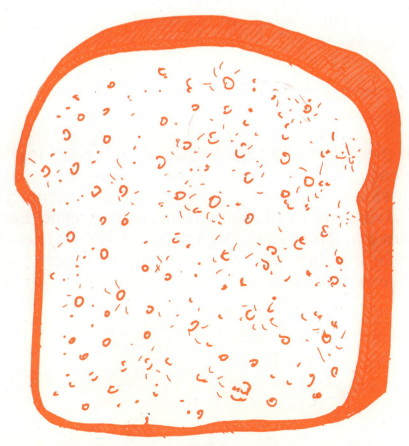

FRECKLED FRENCH TOAST

Utensils:
>mixing bowl
>fork
>frying pan

Ingredients:
>1 egg
>1 tablespoon milk
>¼ teaspoon cinnamon
>¼ teaspoon vanilla extract
>2 tablespoons butter
>2 slices whole wheat bread
>syrup

Beat the egg, milk, cinnamon and vanilla together in a bowl using a fork.

Melt the butter in a large frying pan over medium heat. Dip each piece of bread into the egg mixture, coating each side well. Lay the egg bread into the warm frying pan and cook until the bottom side is yellow brown (about 1 to 2 minutes). Turn over and cook on the other side for another 1 to 2 minutes. Remove both pieces and serve with your favorite syrup. Serves 1.

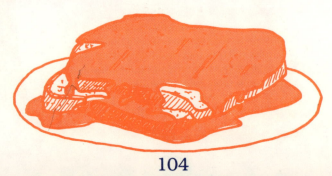

GIANT CREEPING PANCAKE

Utensils:

      dry measuring cup
      measuring spoons
      10-12 inch ovenproof baking dish
      large spoon
      fork or egg beater
      mixing bowl

Ingredients:

      ½ cup flour
      ½ cup milk
      2 eggs
      6 tablespoons margarine
      dash cinnamon
      2 tablespoons lemon juice
      powdered sugar

Beat 2 eggs in bowl. Add ½ cup flour, ½ cup milk and a dash of cinnamon.

Measure the 6 tablespoons butter into a skillet. Melt it. Pour batter into the skillet. Bake for 15 minutes at 375 degrees. Sprinkle with powdered sugar and lemon juice. Bake 5 more minutes. Serve warm.

PRETZEL LETTERS

Utensils:

> baking sheet
> fork
> mixing bowl
> pastry brush

Ingredients:

> 1 16-ounce package frozen bread dough
> 1 egg white
> 1 teaspoon water
> coarse salt

Thaw the bread in its original wrapping in your refrigerator overnight.

Flour hands well. Divide the dough into 24 pieces. Roll each piece into a long strip. Shape the strips into letters or the traditional pretzel twist.

Place on well-greased baking sheet. Do not crowd. Let these stand covered with a towel for 20 minutes.

Next, beat the egg white and water together with a fork. Using a pastry brush, paint it on the top of the bread. (This will help make them shine and works like glue to make the salt stick.) Use your fingers to sprinkle salt over the glazed bread. Bake at 350 degrees for 20 minutes or until golden brown.

DELICIOUS DRINKS

KID-BITS

LIQUID VOLUME

We most commonly measure liquid volume by pints, quarts and gallons.

> 2 pints equal 1 quart
> 4 quarts equal 1 gallon

We are beginning to measure liquids METRICALLY. The LITER is the basic metric unit of measuring liquid volume.

A liter is slightly more than a quart:

> 1 liter equals 1 quart plus .057 quart

To convert quarts to liters, multiply quarts by .946.

Try this one:

> How many liters is 4 quarts?

ANSWER: 3.784 (4 times .946 equals 3.784)

108

SCHOOL'S OUT PUNCH

Utensils:

mixing bowl
spoon
measuring cup
pitcher
ice-cube trays
bottle opener

Ingredients:

1-quart package strawberry Kool-Aid
1 cup sugar
4 cups water
1 small can frozen lemonade, thawed
    (6-ounce)
1 large can frozen orange juice
2 quart bottles of ginger ale
6-ounce jar maraschino cherries

Mix Kool-Aid, sugar and water. Add the lemonade, orange juice, and pineapple juice. Stir until all is mixed thoroughly. Place cherry in the bottom of each section of the ice-cube tray. Pour punch into the tray and freeze. Store rest of the punch in the refrigerator. When ready to serve, add ginger ale to the punch mixture and serve over the punch ice-cubes. Invite your friends for a party!

INSTANT HOT CHOCOLATE MIX

Utensils:

> mixing bowl
> measuring cup
> spoon
> air-tight container

Ingredients:

> 2½ cups powdered milk
> ¾ cup of powdered cream
> 2 cups of instant chocolate mix
> ¾ cup confectioners' sugar

Stir all ingredients together. Put in air-tight container. When ready to make hot chocolate, add 1 heaping tablespoon to one cup of hot water.

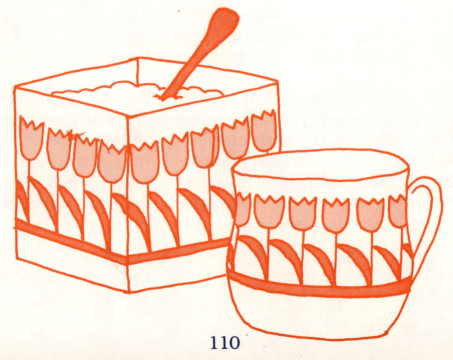